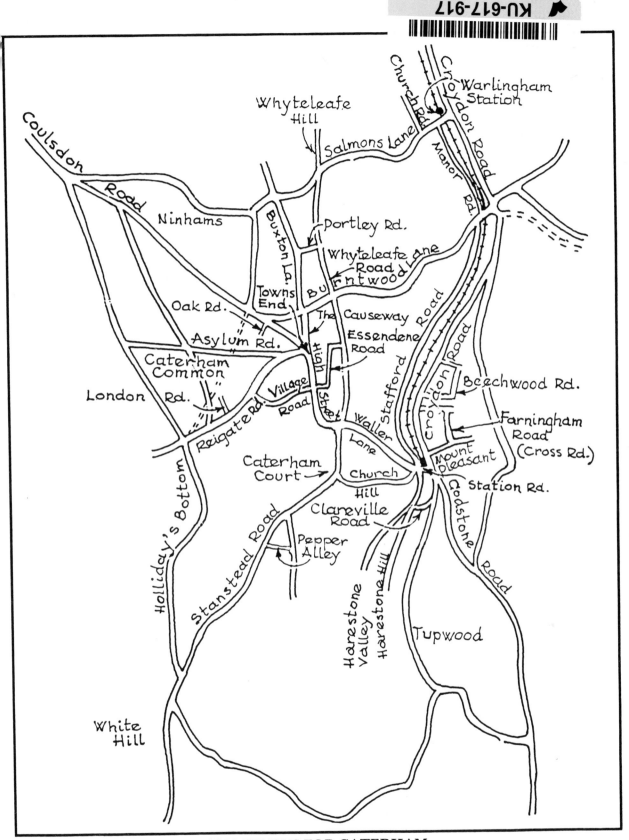

**1881 CENSUS FOR CATERHAM**

# Bygone

# CATERHAM

St Mary's church, 1883.

# Bygone
# CATERHAM

## Jean Tooke

## Phillimore

1988

Published by
PHILLIMORE & CO. LTD.
Shopwyke Hall, Chichester, Sussex

ISBN 0 85033 646 5

Printed and bound in Great Britain by
BIDDLES LTD.
Guildford, Surrey

*To Jeoffry Spence
and the late James Cockburn Batley
whose knowledge and enthusiasm
encouraged my own research*

# List of Illustrations

*Acknowledgements*

The illustrations have been provided from many sources. The majority are treasured family photographs or Edwardian postcards loaned by local collectors. There are also photographs from the extensive collection deposited in Caterham Hill and Valley Libraries through the foresight of former librarian, Charles Silverthorne. I am grateful to the following for permission to reproduce illustrations: L. Alchin 57; J. J. Browne (Jewellers) Ltd. 42, 93, 98, 149; J. Cadle 49, 86, 87, 127, 155; Caterham Clearance Centre 99, 154, 164; Caterham & District Rifle Club 160; Caterham Hill & Valley Libraries 18, 22, 31, 38, 44, 45, 48, 65, 103, 107, 111, 113, 114, 124, 126, 138, 141, 151, 152, 153; Courtauld Institute of Art 132; The Earl Crawford 73; Croydon Health Authority Mental Handicap Unit 120, 121, 122; D. Eyles 52, 53, 56; J. Faulkner 47, 59, 68, 96, 168; D. Frankland 115, 139; J. Gent 20, 25, 29, 50, 117, 173; V. Grant 158; Guy Hewett (Greengrocer) 43; F. Holloway 51, 63, 97; W. Jackson 143; V. Jarrett 35, 128; C. Kearton 146, 147; B. Knight 12, 13, 14, 19, 30, 54, 64, 90, 91, 94, 95, 100, 116, 129, 157, 159, 161; C. Knight 21; J. Knight 9, 15, 16; W. Liversidge 88; M. Martin 78, 79, 84, 85, 131, 134, 135, 136, 166; National Portrait Gallery London 70, 71, 72; Ordnance Survey 2; R. Packham 11, 17, 32, 33, 37, 55, 62, 83, 101, 102, 104, 105, 106, 109, 125, 130, 145, 167; L. Page 165; J. Ratcliffe 118; E. Rendell 92; St Mary's Church Archives 108; K. Sandiford 40; W. Sharpe 58; N. Skinner 7; J. Spence 1, 10, 24, 61; H. Street 4, 5; D. Symonds 142; G. Toms 66, 67, 140, 144, 156; R. Wheeldon 6, 8, 39, 80, 81, 82, 110, 112, 150, 168; P. Wilkinson 36, 162, 163.

Assistance and advice have also been given by Pam Blanking, Michael Cranmer, Margaret Duck, Frank Freedman and Bruce Males; John Janaway, Senior Librarian, Surrey Local Studies Library; local librarians John Lemans, Catherine Pearce and Bridget Revell; Lloyds Bank PLC and the House of Commons Library. Information on the *Commonwealth Tavern* has been received from Herbert Shaw and Allied Breweries Ltd. and on Goss china from the Central Library, Hanley. Grahame Brooks, Bourne Society Photographic Group Leader, has not only taken the cover photograph and plate No. 46, but given invaluable advice on the illustrations.

## Select Bibliography

Baldwin, J., *Caterham Bowling Club 1911-86*

Batley, J. C. (ed.), *A Jubilee History of Caterham and Warlingham*

Binns, M. E., *North Downs Church*

Blomfield, E. de C., *A Century at Caterham 1884-1984*

Bourne Society, *Bulletins nos. 1-128*

Bourne Society, *Local History Records Vols I-XXVI*

Bourne Society, *Then and Now*

Burrell, K., *Happy Days*

Caterham Hill Congregational Church, *Centenary Souvenir 1976*

Caterham Valley Library Local History Collection: Gaskin, W., *Caterham and the Guards*; Toms, G., *Recollections of a Village Community*; Treleavan, R., *Caterham Churches and Population Growth 1851-1914*

Gibson, J., *St Lawrence's Hospital 1870-1956*

Marshall, J., *History of the Parish Church of St John the Evangelist*

Saaler, P., *The Houses of Caterham Valley 1868-1939*

Saaler, P., *The Soldiers of Caterham 1914-1918*

St John Ambulance (Caterham Division), *75 Years of Service 1896-1971*

Spence, J., *The Caterham Railway*

Spence, J., *St Mary's Church 1866-1966*

Spence, J., *The Old Parish Church of St Lawrence*

Stewart, R. L., *The Catholic Church in Caterham 1879-1979*

Swift, R. C., *Methodism in the Purley Circuit*

Tooke, J. and Packham R., *Caterham in Old Picture Postcards*

Turk, N. and Charman, G., *Cricket in Caterham 1767-1973*

# On the Hill

In 1851 census enumerator James Balch noted 487 inhabitants occupying 92 houses in the North Downs parish of Caterham. Although its 2,460 acres included the Valley, the majority of houses were situated on the Hill near the tiny church, rectory and Caterham Court. The villagers were tradesmen or agricultural labourers working for tenant farmers and bailiffs as there was no resident Lord of the Manor.

Ten years later, City businessmen living in grand mansions in Stanstead Road overlooking the Valley were included in the count, but the most far-reaching changes were apparent in the 1881 census returns. A total population of 6,258 was reported, with 4,445 living on the Hill. By that time both the massive Metropolitan Asylum and the Guards Depot had opened. Farm and common land had been replaced by small villas and terraced houses for Asylum workers. High Street houses had been converted to shops and there seemed to be a public house on every corner. Newcomers, like blacksmith Robert Vigar, had expanded their businesses as the town grew. Although the newly developed Valley was less than half a mile away, the community on the Hill was self-contained, for the dangerously steep and unlit Waller Lane and Church Hill were a barrier to communication.

During the next 30 years new estates were laid out including the extensive Nineham's estate. Assistant overseer William Brind estimated at the 1910 Licensing Sessions that seven-eighths of the Asylum staff lived within the vicinity of the *Golden Lion*. Their neighbours included army pensioners, domestic servants, Croydon and City commuters. The census figures collected the next year confirmed this growth. Out of Caterham's population of 10,849, there were 7,138 people living on the Hill. The small village had been transformed to a country town.

1.  Caterham Court with its 400 acres was owned, occupied and farmed by the Rowed family between 1730 and 1790 after which it was leased to successive tenants. It stood on the crest of Great Hill (Church Hill) with commanding views across the Valley. This photograph, taken about 1910, shows the original Georgian house with the Victorian west wing on the left.

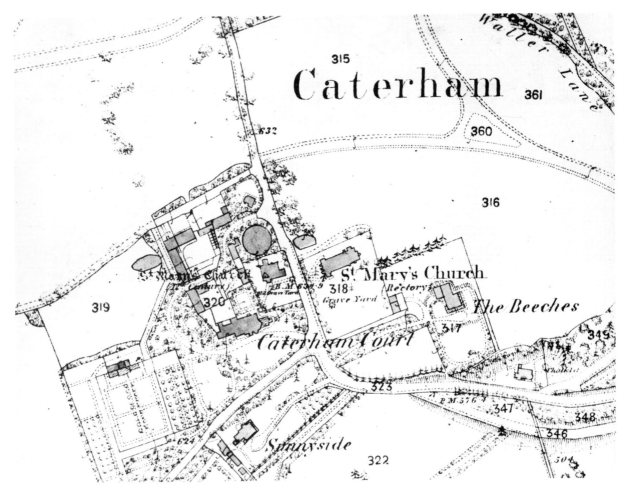

2.   On this 1868 Ordnance Survey map Caterham Court, its walled garden, outbuildings, dew ponds and carriage drive can be seen. Note that both the ancient and newly-built (1866) parish churches, surrounded by their small graveyards, are named St Mary's church. 'Rectory' does not indicate the building but refers to the type of tithes collected. Sunnyside has been renamed Lynton Croft.

3.   Woodside, Stanstead Road, situated in a splendid position on the hillside with breathtaking views across the Valley, was one of the first houses to be built on the Caterham Manor estate in 1861. After the Street family moved there in 1881, a fine 40ft. music room was added, its stage large enough for two grand pianos and a string quartet.

4. Joseph Edward Street (1840-1908), an underwriter, was elected Chairman of Lloyds in 1903. A founder member of the Bach Choir in 1876 and Secretary of the Madrigal Society, he was also President of the Caterham Choral Society. He would act as accompanist at their well-reviewed concerts in the Public Hall, the chorus numbering over 100 voices. He is photographed with his youngest son Edmund, a gifted violinist who studied at the Berlin Musik Hofschule.

5. Florrie and her small sister May Street, granddaughters of Joseph Edward Street, accompanied by Margaret Hilliard, a musical friend, are walking by the side of the field on the Woodside estate. Nos. 25-29 Stanstead Road are built on the field, while Nos. 1-3 Woodside Close are situated in the meadow lower down the hill.

6. In 1851 farm labourers with their large families lived in the Pepper Alley cottages (Harestone Lane). This one surviving cottage has now been extended and carefully restored.

7. Lashmar Cottages (now demolished) adjoining *The Harrow* were believed to be the original public house. On 9 June 1846 William Lashmar, an Oxted brewer, paid the Manorial Court one shilling and threepence 'according to the custom of the Manor' when 'messuages and garden called *the Old Harrow*, situate at Platts Green, held at yearly rent of threepence' were transferred to him.

8. 'How do you like the house – is it not splendid' was the message on this 1906 postcard. This could have equally applied to the immaculate coach house and stables behind The Buckstones, Buxton Lane. According to his obituary in 1910, shipbroker Harvie Mitchell, a well-known cross country rider noted for his horses and smart carriages, 'looked upon the innovation of the motor car with disdain'.

9. Harvie Mitchell's horses would have been shoed at the blacksmith's forge on the left. The High Street, photographed about 1895, is almost deserted. On the right is the Fire Engine House with its small bell turret. In the distance are covered wagons outside the *Blacksmiths Arms*.

10. The *Old Blacksmiths Arms*, opened in 1820, was sketched by Frederick Bradbury Winter in 1877. The following year it was demolished after brewers A. C. & S. Crowley, who had taken a 99-year lease, built for £2,000 the present public house on an adjoining site.

11. Delivery day at the *Blacksmiths Arms*, about 1906, was captured by High Street photographer Fenton. Smoking concerts and exhibition billiard matches were arranged in the large club room by Mr. D. Chalmers, licensee from 1901 to 1908. On Wednesday and Saturday afternoons, changing accommodation and teas were provided for football teams after their matches in the nearby Rectory field.

12. *Ye Olde King and Queen* did not become a beerhouse until 1845, although there is evidence that it is an 18th-century building. By 1910 it was owned by Page & Overton, the Croydon brewery. The three small children standing together are George Ibbotson (left) and Cyril Vigar (centre), grandsons of blacksmith Robert Vigar, and Henry King (right).

13.  Robert Vigar was an expert blacksmith, listing on his trade card the wide range of services essential for a country community. Charging ninepence an hour, he would sharpen chaff knives and saws, grind scissors and shears, solder zinc baths and fish kettles and even provide Viscountess Sherbrooke with a tin tray for her parrot cage.

14.  The reverse side of Robert Vigar's trade card listed his achievements in shoeing competitions at agricultural shows, including the prestigious Royal Agricultural Society's Show. After his admission to the Worshipful Company of Farriers, its coat of arms was included on this card.

15. Blacksmith Robert Vigar's workmen, wearing traditional leather aprons, stand outside Townend forge *c.*1903. Jesse Bridger is third left. The land for the forge and adjoining house were purchased for £320 in 1883. Iron wheelplates, cartwheels and rollers are in evidence. The contracts included shoeing Lion, Kitty, Traveller, Turp and Tippler, the Metropolitan Asylum's farm horses (*see* 123).

16.   Henrietta Vigar (right) and her younger sister Emma (centre), photographed with the maid, Ethel Ashdown, served in their father's ironmonger's shop (now Peters Stores). In 1903 the windows were crammed with garden implements, hurricane lamps, saucepans, colanders, funnels and a row of assorted teapots. An advertising board for carriers Carter Paterson is propped up against the wall.

17.   R. T. 'Tom' Vigar, the blacksmith's son, opened his Trusty Motor and Cycle Works next to the *Royal Oak*. Behind the double doors, on the right, was a pit used for motor and motor cycle repairs. Local agent for Singer cycles, he also built bicycles to customers' specifications.

18.   Family butcher, Mr. H. Sheargold, photographed by Kent & Fenton outside his shop at 22 High Street, may have been taking part in the 1901 Fanciers' Show Horse Parade (*see* 142). The Tradesmen's Annual Bank Holiday Sports were held in his field, now Hillcroft School playing fields.

19. This advertisement appeared in the 1908 *Guide to Caterham*. Moving to Caterham in 1878, William Brind worked as foreman for builder William Thompson. Appointed Assistant Overseer and Rate Collector by the Parish Council in 1897, he held this position until his death in 1923. A popular and public spirited man, he was Horticultural Society Secretary from 1892 until 1911 (*see* 66).

20. George and Herbert Bunce are photographed in the garden studio behind their parents' house, North Lodge, Westway. The next year, 1906, they moved to newly-built Langdale Studios, No. 26 Westway. Specialising in Guards' Depot photographs, they also took innumerable studio portraits, wedding groups, social events and local views, including the *Westway* series reproduced on postcards.

21.  Local children are attentively watching the itinerant knife grinder at work outside Bunce Bros. Westway studios. In this splendid photograph, taken on the spur of the moment by George Bunce in 1928, are left to right: – Connolly, Les Vinten, George Kearns, Sid Gasson, – King, Den Miles and Don Vinten, with Cyril, David and Marjorie Knight standing in the road outside their house, No. 31 Westway.

22.  Waller Lane, a steep and stony road, was the quickest route from the Hill to the Valley. Although seats were provided by the Parish Council in 1895, the message on this 1908 postcard reads 'the view may look all right but when one has to climb it after coming down on the last train, it's anything but pleasant, I can assure you'.

# Living in the Valley

*The Half Moon Inn* near Wapses Lodge, White Knobs Farm, quarrymen's and limeworkers' cottages at Tupwood or the Godstone Road chalkpit were the only buildings in the Valley in 1851. This dramatically changed when Caterham Railway opened in 1856 and railway director George Drew, together with his son, George Henry Drew, purchased the Lordship of Caterham Manor in 1858. Concerned at empty trains, they proceeded to build grand mansions on manorial land, first on the prime hillside sites with superb views and then in the newly constructed Harestone Valley Road. Purchasers of estates in 1866 were not allowed 'to make bricks for sale, make lime nor use buildings for any trade except farmer, nurseryman, market gardener or hotel keeper nor build a dwelling house of less value than £800'.

Wealthy bankers, stockbrokers, underwriters, merchants and shipowners moved into the Valley to escape the unpleasant London fogs, either commuting daily or spending weekends in their country 'cottages', with names such as Woodside, Lamorna or Kilmarnock reflecting local features, childhood homes or Scottish towns. Designed by architects Philip Webb, John Sulman and Richard Martin, residences were built to clients' high standards by William Thompson. Attractive lodges were added for outdoor staff. However, their huge size created long term problems for, as early as 1910 when it was proving difficult to sell Harestone and other mansions, the *Caterham Weekly Press* suggested that smaller villas should be built in their extensive grounds.

Villas had been built in Godstone Road, on railway company land in Croydon Road, while, on the Commonwealth estate, workmen's dwellings appeared in Farningham and Commonwealth Roads for railway and building workers whose sons and daughters became housemaids, gardeners and grooms.

By 1881, the Valley and Hill populations were almost equal. Thirty years later, in 1911, the proportion was the same although the population had nearly doubled. However the Valley had become the business centre, for the bank and post office were situated opposite the station and, after a tremendous battle between Hill and Valley tradesmen, Soper Hall was erected in Harestone Valley Road.

23.   Harestone Valley *c.*1876, showing Harestone House on the left. Built in 1860, leased by Australian Henry Greenaway, it was demolished after Harestone was built on the adjoining field in front of the line of trees. The three gentlemen's residences, left to right, are Underwood built in 1868, Alleyne in 1876 and Orchardleigh in 1874. Note the saplings planted in their gardens.

24. Harestone, photographed from Church Hill above Brabourne, was designed by architect John Sulman for William Garland Soper in 1879. No expense was spared on its exterior or luxurious interior. On the left are the stables leading to the cowman's cottage in Colburn Avenue, then a carriage drive, while the gardener's cottage seen here is in Harestone Valley Road.

25. The popular Edwardian game of croquet is being played on the immaculate Harestone lawns in summer 1906. A tennis court is marked out on the right in front of the conservatory. This postcard by Alec Braid, with *x* indicating 'Auntie', was sent to South Africa where the Soper family had profitable business interests.

26.  The iron railings in Harestone Valley Road, bordering the large meadow on the right, marked the boundary of the Harestone estate. It extended originally to the junction of Harestone Valley Road and Harestone Hill, but William Garland Soper gave the triangular site for the Congregational church. Mrs. William Kilby, wife of the livery stables proprietor, is seen with her baby son. Behind the high wooden fence are the front gardens of Beechwood.

27.  Beechwood, overlooking Harestone Valley, was conveniently situated opposite the Congregational church. Percy Clarke, who moved there in 1892, was one of the deacons. The garden was the venue for the 1913 Sunday School Treat when 'the main attraction was the cart which careered down the sloping lawn at full speed upsetting its small occupant at the bottom'.

28.  This typical Edwardian dining room, lit by gas, was photographed at Beechwood. Doubtless the ornaments were among nearly 200 wedding presents listed in the *Caterham Free Press* when Percy Clarke married Marion Winter in September 1892. In 1900, Mrs. Clarke advertised for a 'Between Girl about 16 years old for house and kitchen. Cook and Housemaid kept.'

29.  By 1900 Harestone Valley was renowned for its fine houses set in spacious grounds hidden behind magnificent trees. In this panoramic view from fields above Harestone Lane is Bradenhurst, Harestone Hill, on the right, with its extensive kitchen gardens (now Bradenhurst Close). To the left is the patterned roof of Kilmarnock and far left Shandon Cottage, Loxford Road. The three houses in Harestone Valley Road are, left to right, Briarmount, Yew House (now demolished) and Allestree.

30. William Thompson, advertising in the 1908 Guide, was a builder specialising in high quality work. The Victorian mansions are his memorial. Established in 1873 with yards and workshops in Croydon Road, 34 men and six boys were employed in the business by 1881. An enlightened employer, he not only trained his men well, but provided them with generous sickness and funeral benefits through his Shop Club Fund (*see* 114).

31.  Quarryman Albert Elliff Hills, baptised in the parish church in 1844, is standing outside Marden Cottage, Tupwood, where he was born, with his wife and daughter, his musical instruments and caged birds. He was the third generation to work in the quarries. Among his numerous cousins were the Rayner Hill family, Caterham Valley nurserymen and bootshop proprietors.

32.  By 1904 Croydon Road had been developed. This view from the slopes above Stafford Road looks towards the two detached houses in Elgin Crescent, with smaller cottages lower down the hill in Beechwood Road. The houses, shops and builders' yards in the foreground from No. 201 Croydon Road on the left, to Ashdene on the right, backed on to the railway line obscured by trees in this photograph.

Stafford Road, Caterham.

33. In 1914 Stafford Road, running parallel to the railway line, was a private road with gates at each end. It was little more than a carriage drive to the large houses situated between Church Hill and Burntwood Lane – Stafford House, Holmwood, Beechlands and Warlingham Grange.

34. Holmwood, Stafford Road, was auctioned in June 1901 following the death of Alfred Savill Tompkins (see 135). A grain merchant and captain in the Volunteers, he had trained samoyed dogs at Holmwood in preparation for the 1898 *Southern Cross* Antarctic Expedition. The property was bought by William Morcom who lived there until his death in 1934. The house has been demolished but the lodge can still be seen.

## Sales by Auction.

By order of Trustees.—In the lovely Caterham Valley.

A particularly choice FREEHOLD PROPERTY, comprising an excellent Modern Residence, containing 10 bed and dressing rooms, bath, four fine reception-rooms, and excellent offices; capital stabling; model farmery; productive kitchen garden, tennis lawn, conservatory, greenhouse, paddock, &c., in all about seven acres; within a few minutes of the station.— Messrs.

ARBER, RUTTER, WAGHORN and BROWN will OFFER the above Charming PROPERTY, known as Holmwood, Stafford-road Caterham, for SALE, by AUCTION, at the Mart, Tokenhouse-yard, City, E.C., on THURSDAY, June 12, 1901, at one o'clock precisely.

Printed particulars, with photo and conditions of sale, may be had of Messrs. Greenfield and Cracknell, solicitors, 3, Lancaster-place Strand, W.C.; at the Mart: and with order to view at the auctioneers offices, 1, Mount-street, London, W.

35.   William Morcom, a City paper manufacturer, is sitting in his carriage outside Holmwood with his smartly attired coachman Charles Jarrett *c*.1905. Knighted in 1925 for 'political and local services', Sir William had first represented the East Ward on the Urban District Council in 1906. In 1915 he was elected Chairman of the Council in May and appointed a Justice of the Peace in July.

36.   Sylva House, Waller Lane, demolished in 1948, was lent by the Asprey family to Belgian refugees in 1914. Before then it was the residence of tea broker John Shepard (*see* 109). George Davis, William Garland Soper's father-in-law, who built the first Congregational chapel on land opposite the house, lived there in 1865. When Sir William Morcom, a Cornishman by birth, bought the house for his daughter Mrs. Savill, it was renamed Lamorna.

# Shopping in the Valley

Grocer George Lee was the only Valley retailer named in Kelly's 1862 Directory, but by 1881, census enumerator Edward Harris, the prosperous Godstone Road saddler, listed at least 30 business premises in the vicinity of the railway station. Linen drapers, dress, mantle and bootmakers, clothiers, corndealers and a chemist had opened to serve the new wealthy residents while the Co-operative Industrial Society Stores catered for the less affluent. As the town grew, new shopping parades were built. By 1914, there were nearly 100 family businesses and one multiple store, the International Tea Company Stores.

The Surrey Hills had been discovered by visitors, day trippers and cyclists who purchased postcards and inexpensive souvenirs. Dining and tea rooms and three public houses, the *Commonwealth Tavern*, *Greyhound* and *Old Surrey Hounds*, advertised facilities for 'pic-nic parties and cycling clubs'. The temperance *Coffee Tavern*, opened in 1880, provided overnight accommodation while weekly boarders stayed at the *Railway Hotel*, completely rebuilt in 1902.

37. In 1878 the few Croydon Road shops backed on to the railway. Far left is the *Greyhound* adjoining John White, jeweller, with blacksmith Tremain in the centre and the Co-operative Industrial Society Stores on the right. Across the railway, from left to right, are The Priory, the first Congregational chapel (now Stafford Hall), The Garlands (L. M. Beasley & Co. Ltd.) and Sylva House.

38. By 1890 there were businesses both sides of the Croydon Road. It was narrow and flinty, noted for its clouds of dust in dry weather. The shops on the left adjoining the livery stables were later pulled down. On the right is Sandiford's fruit and provision stores. The detached three-storey building was opened in 1880 as a residential *Coffee Tavern* with shops at street level.

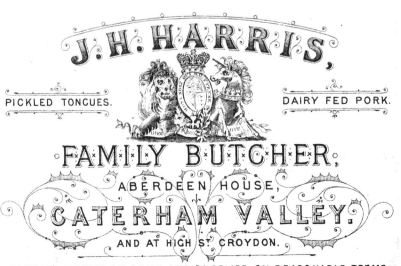

J. H. HARRIS,

PICKLED TONGUES.          DAIRY FED PORK.

FAMILY BUTCHER,

ABERDEEN HOUSE,

CATERHAM VALLEY.

AND AT HIGH ST. CROYDON.

FAMILIES WAITED ON DAILY AND SUPPLIED ON REASONABLE TERMS.

39. In January 1887 butcher J. H. Harris rented a lean-to shop by Kilby's livery stables (seen in plate 38), at a time when there was a series of thefts from butchers' open counters. According to the *Croydon Chronicle*, he was fortunate, for with the help of fishmonger Mr. Turner he managed to 'detect, chase and catch the slippery eel', a local coachman who had stolen a prime Welsh mutton joint.

40. Butcher R. G. Knight opened in June 1901 underneath the *Coffee Tavern*. After bullocks had been purchased from the royal farms, the royal coat of arms was placed over the doorway and Prince of Wales feathers between the first floor windows! His Christmas display was so well stocked that a night watchman had to be hired to protect it.

41. Knight's advertisements in the *Caterham Weekly Press* were always topical (*see* 84 & 85). At Christmas the popular competition for judging the weight of a bullock purchased from the London Cattle Show would be advertised, with prizes of £1, 15s. and 10s. awarded. In 1907 it was reported that 'his customers are becoming adepts' as seven customers guessed the weight at 800½ pounds.

42. The manageress, Miss Wingate, is photographed with her male assistants and delivery boy in about 1913, outside the International Stores, the first multiple store to open in the Valley. Situated next to R. G. Knight, it stood at the corner of Mount Pleasant and Croydon Road.

43. Greengrocer Guy Hewett, now at No. 20 Croydon Road, is the oldest surviving business in the Valley. Standing in the doorway of the first shop, No. 103 Croydon Road, opened in 1879, is proprietor Hannah Hewett with daughter Gertrude. Outside is husband George and 10-year-old son Guy who in 1889 when this photograph was taken already had his own colourful delivery cart.

44. From 1898 to 1909, Cornishman Alec Braid was the influential editor of the *Caterham Free Press*, renamed *Caterham Weekly Press* in 1901, in which he chronicled in detail activities of the growing community. An expert photographer, he published many local views including the first coloured postcards in 1904, selling them at his shop, No. 47 Croydon Road.

45. Alec Braid, seated right, sold the *Caterham Weekly Press* to the *Surrey Mirror* publishers, the Holmesdale Press, Redhill Junction, whose staff are pictured here in 1905. He remained editor until December 1909 when he was presented with a testimonial by the appreciative readers.

46. This 50mm.-high *Bridlington Elizabethan Quart Measure* with its handpainted Caterham Urban District Council coat of arms was manufactured by W. H. Goss. Although Alec Braid advertised the sale of Caterham arms china in June 1904, Goss heraldic porcelain china would have been sold by the sole agents, the Fancy Stores, No. 22 Croydon Road, to summer visitors as an inexpensive souvenir.

47. In 1910 coffee, lunches and teas were served to cyclists by Mr. W. R. Horwell at his Refreshment Rooms, No. 19 Godstone Road. Cycling clubs would have been able to pre-book the private dining room on the right. On the wall above the window, a board advertises Tremain, the blacksmith's shop next to the refreshment rooms.

48.  Lloyd, Barnett and Bosanquet Bank's first branch in 1886 was a room in Surrey Hills Estate Agency on the left. In 1890 the present bank house was built in Station Avenue, dated by the rainhead between the second-floor windows. Banking business was transacted on the ground floor, the manager living on the upper two floors.

49.  The nursery and florist's concern, with greenhouses at the side and gardens behind, can be seen in the previous photograph, between the Surrey Hills Estate Agency and Lloyd's Bank. This advertisement, inserted by Rayner Hill, appeared in a 1913 Caterham guide promoting the town's attractions.

50. The first *Railway Hotel*, opened in 1856, was similar in design to the railway station and livery stables. It was demolished in 1902 when a new hotel was built in its gardens. The Grand Parade on the same site is dated 1903. When this photograph was taken in 1900, the shops in Godstone Road included a butcher with the striped awning and bootmaker Allen Rayner Hill on the corner.

51.   The *Railway Hotel*, rebuilt by licensee George Payne, was renowned for its attractive gardens which featured a fountain, rose pergola, croquet lawn and tennis courts. Lined up outside the station.are the horse-drawn hackney carriages licensed by the Urban District Council. Regulations included a maximum speed of five miles per hour.

52.   The staff at the *Railway Hotel* are photographed in the Palm Court in 1902. This group includes the hall porter and three chambermaids in spotless white starched aprons. The two barmaids including Emma Parker (second left) are wearing smart black dresses.

53.  This charming photograph was taken in the *Railway Hotel* bar by postman Alec Wright soon after the hotel was built in 1902. Emma Parker, the barmaid, is seen with her fiancé , postman James Barber.

54. Corndealer George Ashby's premises were at the corner of The Square and Timber Hill. They were originally occupied by sub-postmaster Edward Pollard, with post office business transacted at the rear of his clothier's shop. In 1898 the sub-post office was transferred to a grocery store in Godstone Road.

55. Caterham Valley Post Office moved to the corner of newly-built Grand Parade and Occupation Row (Church Walk) on 19 February 1904. Conveniently situated opposite the station for despatching and collecting mail, the sorting office was in the basement. The telephone exchange, opened on 22 October, was on the first floor. Note the appropriately named Frosts Stores (*see* 63).

56.   Postmaster Adolph Hahn with his staff *c*.1908. Standing in the middle row, from left to right: postman Alec Wright, messenger boy Bert Crewe, postmen James Barber, his uncle Benjamin, father William and Frank Allum. When William Barber retired in 1909 after 40 years' service, he estimated that he had walked over 200,000 miles.

57. Among the staff standing outside the present Post Office, opened in October 1910 at a cost of £2,000, is messenger boy Oliver Alchin with his bicycle. The mailcarts were pushed from the station, through the double doors on the left and up by lift to the spacious sorting office. On the first floor was the telephone exchange.

58. Croydon Road, photographed from St John's church tower, portrays a thriving shopping centre surrounded by tree-lined hills. The open-topped 59A omnibus from Stockwell is passing the derelict site of the *Old Surrey Hounds*. Destroyed by fire in 1916, it was completely rebuilt (*see* 93).

# Transport

On 1 January 1900, the new Caterham station opened at the end of the recently laid double track from Purley. More frequent trains were promised in the timetable. Before then, passengers' interests seemed secondary to the wrangling between the London, Brighton & South Coast and South-Eastern Railway Companies. In spite of frequent petitions, scandalous court cases, a disapproving letter in *The Times* and vitriolic letters to the *Caterham Free Press*, trains were regularly late and connections frequently missed. It is not surprising that the proposed Coulsdon & Upper Caterham Railway terminating at Willey Heath was supported by Caterham Vestry in 1883.

This disinterest in passenger traffic may have been due to the original plans of the Caterham Railway directors, for the 4½-mile single line had been opened on 4 May 1856 to transport stone from Godstone and Tupwood quarries. When this proved impossible, further plans were made to extend the line to the quarries or link up with other railway lines, for there were few potential customers living in the vicinity.

Gradually trains were filled with passengers living in houses on railway company land, Metropolitan Asylum visitors, guardsmen stationed at the Depot and day trippers visiting the Surrey Hills. Seaside excursions were arranged, while in 1909, after representations from the Tradesmen's Association, cheap tickets were issued on Wednesday afternoons. Beanfeasters from South London visited the town on horse drawn brakes. By 1914 residents owned motor cars, motorised charabancs could be hired, so garages began to replace livery stables. In that year, passengers were able to choose their transport for, at Easter, the first open-topped omnibus from Stockwell, via Purley, arrived in Caterham Valley.

59.   The station forecourt, on the left, was built in 1900 after the railway line from Purley was doubled. Station Avenue was widened and the roadway raised. The small feeder pillar, on the right, caused an outcry when it appeared in August 1903. At a special Council meeting, it was finally agreed to allow 'the obnoxious obstruction' to remain, provided the Urban Electric Supply Co. 'painted it a nice colour and placed a light on the top'.

60.   Before 1900, Caterham station was located on the site of Waitrose Supermarket. Successive stationmasters were popular with commuters although the railway company was not. When Mr. Foweraker was transferred to Lewisham in 1894, the *Caterham Free Press* reported that 'it was only to be expected that the residents and tradesmen would present him with a testimonial'.

61.   The empty train on the right is preparing to leave the sidings. When the track from Purley was doubled, a new central platform and signal box was built at Caterham. Although the Urban Electric Supply Company's chimney is prominent, the station was still lit by gas when this photograph was taken *c*.1910.

62. By 1867 carriages, landaus, barouches, wagonettes and horse-drawn brakes could be hired from Kilby's Livery Stables in the station yard. City commuters' horses and gigs would be left there for the day. The proprietor, jobmaster Thomas Kilby, was at one time employed as a groom by George Henry Drew at Essendene. His sons carried on the business.

63. George Tester, operating one of the Council's horse-drawn snow ploughs outside Kilby's Livery Stables in 1910, is attempting to clear Croydon Road. The Urban District Council owned three similar machines purchased from the Bristol Wagon Co. for £11 each (see 55).

64.  Blacksmith Robert Vigar opened a second forge in the Valley, conveniently situated next to Kilby's Livery Stables in Croydon Road. It was managed by his son-in-law, George Ibbotson, on the right. A champion farrier, he won many prizes at agricultural shows.

65.  Regular customers from the *Old Surrey Hounds* are setting off for a day's outing in 1910. The four-horse brake may have been hired from Kilby's Livery Stables or from Thomas Alchin's 'Old Established Livery & Bait Stables' behind the public house.

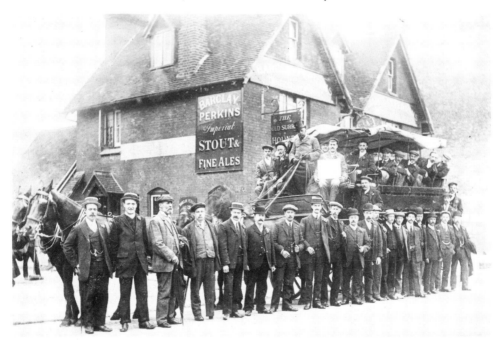

66. By contrast, Horticultural Society members hired a motor charabanc for their Derby Day outing, probably in 1911. On the front seat are Joe Whilock, *Tally Ho* licensee and outing organiser (left), William Brind (centre) and William Toms (right). *See* 140.

67. Sitting proudly in their Lagonda car in 1906 are William Toms, his wife and small son, William, in their garden at Heathview, Banstead Road (now Napier Court). A well-known nurseryman, whose business was later continued by his sons, William and George, he was a keen Horticultural Society member, Surrey County bowls player and Chairman of Caterham Urban District Council in 1925.

68.  The County Garage (Layhams Garage), Croydon Road, occupied the site of the *Half Moon Inn*. Like its predecessor, a coaching inn, it provided a necessary service, although not accommodation, for travellers on the London-Eastbourne road.

69.  A horse and cart has stopped outside the entrance to the County Garage & Motor Works with its AA sign displayed. The only other traffic in this deserted Croydon Road is a steam roller in the distance. On the right is a footpath signposted to Woldingham station.

# A Political Gallery

Members of Parliament and prospective parliamentary candidates were attracted to the district. Its proximity to Westminster, the new railway line and healthy climate encouraged them to buy estates. This was most fortunate. Usually of independent means, successful in their careers and public spirited by inclination, they played an active part in community affairs.

Banker Edward Brodie Hoare, churchwarden from 1876 until he became Conservative M.P. for Hampstead in 1888, lived at St Bernards, Whyteleafe Road. From 1902 to 1913, garden parties were held in the grounds in aid of Dr. Barnado's Homes or the Congregational church during the residence of George Croydon Marks, a Cornish Liberal M.P. The most distinguished Liberal to visit the district was William Ewart Gladstone who, when Prime Minister, planted a tree in the grounds of Sherbrooke, Salmons Lane. Robert Lowe, his Chancellor of the Exchequer, later created Viscount Sherbrooke, must have entertained him in some style, for his staff in 1871 included both a French and an English cook.

As a result of 19th-century parliamentary reforms, local landowners could no longer be sure of a local seat. Viscount Balcarres, educated at The Dean School, Underwood Road (now Trundle), was M.P. for Chorley, near Haigh Hall, the family estate in Lancashire. However, in the East Surrey constituency, the Hon. Granville Leveson Gower of Titsey Place was defeated at the 1871 election.

In 1885, Caterham was fitted into the newly formed, oddly shaped Wimbledon constituency, made up of small East Surrey towns, skirting Wandsworth and Croydon. National elections created tremendous local interest and crowded political meetings. In 1910 when the Rt. Hon. Henry Chaplin, Wimbledon's Conservative M.P. spoke at the Public Hall, Godstone Road, seating 1,000, there was standing room only. These meetings would be arranged and financed by local political organisations, for by 1914 the Conservative & Unionist Association, Primrose League, Liberal Association and Socialist Society were listed in local directories and their meetings reported in great detail in the *Caterham Weekly Press*.

70. Robert Lowe (1811-92), a leading Liberal, was Chancellor of the Exchequer 1868-73. He moved to Sherbrooke in 1858, living there until his death 34 years later. Born in Bingham, Nottinghamshire, he was an Australian Member of Parliament 1843-50. Returning to England in 1850, he became M.P. successively for Kidderminster, Calne and London University until created Viscount Sherbrooke of Warlingham in 1880. Cartoon by Harry Furniss.

71.  Edward Brodie Hoare (1841-1911), Conservative M.P. for Hampstead 1888-1902, was appointed a director of Lloyd's Bank after the family banking firm, Barnett, Hoare, Hanbury and Lloyd, was taken over in 1884. During his tenure as churchwarden, the south aisle and chancel, tower and spire were added to St Mary's church. He generously contributed £325 to the building fund.

72.  George Croydon Marks (1858-1938) was an authority on patent laws and a consulting engineer who designed cliff railways. He was Liberal M.P. for Cornish constituencies 1906-24, promoting nonconformist causes in Parliament. Admitted a Caterham Congregational church member in July 1902, he took a particular interest in the small Mission Hall on the Hill. A local magistrate, he was knighted for political services in 1911 and created Baron Marks of Woolwich in 1929.

73.  The 27th Earl of Crawford (1871-1940). In 1881, nine-year-old Viscount Balcarres, later educated at Eton and Oxford, was one of 20 boarders at The Dean School. A distinguished public figure, he was Unionist Chief Whip before he succeeded to the earldom in 1913. Concerned that the arts should be freely available to ordinary men and women, he revitalised moribund national museums. The 1926 Crawford Report led to the establishment of the British Broadcasting Corporation.

74.  The Rt. Hon. Henry Chaplin (1840-1923), known as 'the farmers' friend' and owner of the 1867 Derby winner Hermit, was a Cabinet minister in Lord Salisbury's governments. Selected in 1907 as Conservative and Tariff Reform candidate for the safe Wimbledon seat, he comfortably beat the Hon. Bertrand Russell, first Women's Suffrage candidate, in the ensuing by-election. He was created Viscount Chaplin in 1916.

# Local Government

National government followed party lines in the 19th century, but local government could not. In Caterham there was no elected governing body until the first Parish Council met on 2 January 1895. Before that date local affairs were organised by the parish vestry established in Elizabethan times. Originally a meeting of inhabitants, summoned by a notice nailed on the church door to discuss church business, the vestry had gradually assumed responsibility for parish matters, levying the necessary rates. Churchwardens, overseers responsible for collecting the poor rate and waywardens who surveyed, built and maintained roads were elected. Between 1842 and 1872, the unpopular office of constable responsible for law and order was reluctantly filled by a tradesman such as blacksmith Robert Vigar.

At this time attendance at vestry meetings, rarely exceeding 30 inhabitants, included the new wealthy residents whatever their religion, such as Congregationalist William Garland Soper. Elected overseers now represented the parish on the Godstone Board of Guardians set up in 1834, when 14 parishes amalgamated to form the Godstone Union, while waywardens sat on the Godstone Highway Board established in 1862. These bodies levied, collected and spent the rates. As Caterham's population and rateable value grew, outstripping the other 13 parishes, so did the grievances. Ratepayers considered that their rates subsidised smaller parishes. Dissatisfied with the state of roads, they passed a resolution in 1869 'to sever the connection with Godstone Highway Board'. The vestry implemented parliamentary legislation. The School Board was set up in 1871, the Fire Brigade in 1889, the Burial Board in 1891 and street lighting by gas was approved in 1886.

By 1900 this antiquated and inadequate system of local government had been reorganised. The administrative functions of the traditional Quarter Sessions were transferred to an elected Surrey County Council in 1888. Frederick White of Portley was the town's first county councillor, succeeded in 1891 by William Garland Soper. In 1895 Caterham was allocated seven representatives on the new Godstone Rural District Council. Despite a ratepayers' poll in favour of urban district powers, the vestry was only replaced by a parish council. The fifteen elected councillors in five wards included the Rev. F.A. Bright, St Mary's parish rector and the Rev. J.F.G. Glossop, St Luke's parish vicar. William Garland Soper was co-opted Chairman and Henry Martin appointed Clerk. Although its powers were limited, the parish council co-operated with the 1897 Diamond Jubilee Committee to obtain land for Queen's Park.

Spearheaded by William Garland Soper and supported by *Caterham Free Press* editor, Alec Braid, the town finally became an urban district in 1899, with monthly council meetings at the Masonic Hall, Stafford Road. William Garland Soper was again co-opted first Chairman, architect Henry Martin appointed Surveyor and Sanitary Inspector and solicitor Frederick Bradbury Winter became Clerk to the Council. Godstone Rural District Council claimed compensation for loss of rates but, after a five year legal battle with costs underwritten by William Garland Soper, the House of Lords gave judgment in Caterham's favour in May 1904. A presentation was made to the Chairman by appreciative ratepayers and, after his untimely death in 1908, their donations built the Soper Hall as a memorial to the 'father of modern Caterham'.

75. William Garland Soper J.P. (1837-1908), born in Devon, moved to Caterham in 1866. An influential Congregationalist, he was partner in the South African trading company Davis & Soper and a Master of the Fruiterers' Company. Passionately promoting the town's interests, he became Parish Council Chairman 1895-9 and first Urban District Council Chairman 1899-1908. He was elected a Surrey County Council Alderman in 1901 and Chairman of the Godstone Bench in 1907.

76. This inscribed silver centrepiece and four circular dishes, made by Messrs. Asprey, was presented to William Garland Soper on 8 December 1904, his 67th birthday, 'by the inhabitants of Caterham as a token of appreciation and gratitude for the good work he has rendered during his long residence in their midst'.

77. Although architect Henry Martin's widely approved design for the Soper Hall and Council Offices was published in the *Caterham Weekly Press* on 20 August 1910, only the Memorial Hall, centre, planned as a concert hall and council chamber, and the offices, on the left, were built when it opened in January 1912. The conference hall, on the right, with further offices above, was not added until 1927.

78. Henry Richard Martin (1864-1944) was born in Australia but trained by his uncle, Caterham architect Richard Martin. He designed the Soldiers' Home, Cottage Hospital and Soper Hall. After three years as Clerk to the Parish Council, he was appointed first Surveyor by the Urban District Council in 1899, serving the town's interests loyally and conscientiously. Connected with many local associations, his ability as an organiser was legendary.

# THE DIAMOND JUBILEE.

## *Souvenir Programme*

OF THE

## Caterham Celebrations

### 21st JUNE to 26th JUNE, 1897.

---

Chairman.

W. GARLAND SOPER, J.P.

General Honorary Secretary.

J. D. ROLLS.

Honorary Treasurer.

E. H. COLES.

Executive Committee.

H. R. MARTIN.     H. G. SALMON.

W. SOPER, JUNR.

79.   To celebrate the Diamond Jubilee in 1897, a Bicycle Gymkhana and Public Sports, displays by the Fire Brigade, St John Ambulance and Guards' Depot were held on the Cricket ground (Dene field), with an evening torchlight procession to the bonfire on Gravelly Hill. Schoolchildren were given an entertainment, tea and a Jubilee mug. Old folk enjoyed roast beef and plum pudding in the Public Hall.

# Queen's Park, .. Caterham. . . . .

23rd MAY, 1900.

# Programme.

The Pavilions have been presented by

**HARRY LLOYD, Esq.** and

**WM. GARLAND SOPER, Esq., J.P., C.C.**

The Fountain presented by

**F. A. WHITE, Esq., J.P.**

BRAID. "CATERHAM FREE PRESS."

---

**On Western Cricket Pitch.**

### CRICKET MATCH.

#### Hill v. Valley.

Teams arranged by Mr. W. Brind and Mr. F. W. Wasthage.

---

**6-0 p.m.**

### DISPLAY OF EXHIBITION DRILLS

#### BY CATERHAM FIRE BRIGADE.

**(Under Captain Vigar).**

1. One man Drill.
2. Four men Drill.
3. Six men Turn-out Drill.
4. Four men Drill as No. 1.
5. Six men Wet Drill.

---

**6-30 p.m.**

### PARADE OF DECORATED HORSES AND CARTS, CYCLES, ETC.

The Horses and Carts will parade along the Road in front of the Park and the Cycles around the central walk in the Park.

The following prizes are offered for competition :—

Horses and Carts.

| 1st. | 2nd. | 3rd. | 4th. |
|---|---|---|---|
| £ s. d. | £ s. d. | £ s. d. | £ s. d. |
| 2 10 0 | 1 10 0 | 0 15 0 | 0 7 6 |

Cycles. (No Costumes).

| 1st. | 2nd. | 3rd. |
|---|---|---|
| £ s. d. | £ s. d. | £ s. d. |
| 1 0 0 | 0 10 0 | 0 5 0 |

Lady Edridge and Mrs. E. B. Forbes have kindly consented to act as Judges

---

**7-30 p.m.**

### DISTRIBUTION OF PRIZES BY Mrs. Wm. GARLAND SOPER.

---

**8-0 p.m.**

### ILLUMINATION OF THE PARK.

---

80.  Queen's Park was opened three years after the Diamond Jubilee Committee had requested the Parish Council to 'purchase out of rates recreation grounds as a permanent commemoration'. To secure the site, William Garland Soper bought the 18 acres from the Caterham Park Estate for £1,800, reselling it to the Parish Council in 1898 when the legal formalities had been completed.

81.  After William Garland Soper declared Queen's Park open, the splendid programme organised by Henry Martin was enjoyed by the thousands present, including Board School children. Although the Valley cricket team failed to arrive, the Valley Brass & Reed Band played selections, novelty races were run and Mr. Gibson, the Coulsdon Road grocer, won first prize in the Horse Parade.

82. An inscription in Queen's Park near the Church Road gates reads 'This copper beech tree was planted by Mr. H. R. Martin (Surveyor to the Urban District Council) and Mrs. Martin to commemorate the Relief of Ladysmith on 28th February 1900'.

83. This charming postcard, published by Alec Braid, was sent by a guardsman in 1907. By then, large detached family houses with accommodation for servants had been built in Queen's Park Road. The Dene School, seen behind the trees in Church Road, had moved from Underwood Road.

84 & 85.   In 1909, for the first time at a Council election, local associations sponsored candidates to defeat the 'old time parish clique'. Although Ratepayers' Association Chairman, John Wilkes, organised lively meetings, processions and canvassing, sending a polling card to every elector, he lost by only 35 votes to Tradesmen's Association candidate, Robert Kemp, with landscape gardener Ernest Frost a poor third.

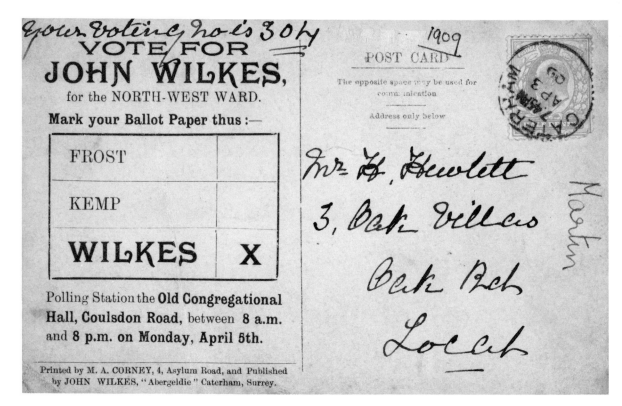

86. & 87. The Urban Electric Supply Company's plan to open its Croydon Road works in 1903 was welcomed and approved by the Urban District Council, but not by Caterham Gas Company, established in 1869 with gasometers in Whyteleafe. An advertising war followed. These advertisements appeared in a 1913 town guide after the Caterham company had become part of the Croydon Gas Company.

88.   Howard Willmott Liversidge J.P. (1869-1934), a barrister who lived at The White Cottage, Whyteleafe Road, was typical of the public-spirited men who contributed so much to Caterham. Successful at the first Urban District Council election in 1899, he represented the north-east ward for 30 years. He was Council Chairman in 1911, and also a Surrey County Councillor 1910-30.

89. On Saturday 24 June 1911, the Caterham Coronation Celebrations Committee entertained 167 elderly residents to a 'Dinner and Variety Entertainment' at the patriotically decorated Public Hall. Percy Broad, the caterer, not only provided roast beef, fruit tarts, jellies and strawberries but sang 'My Dear Old Dutch'. Other acts included a comedian, farmyard mimic, violinist and clever siffleuse.

90. The 1889 Vestry meeting instructed the Overseers to form a Fire Brigade, paying the cost out of the poor rate. Blacksmith Robert Vigar (right) was appointed captain. His uniform cost £5 5s., the firemen's tunics £2 2s., trousers 19s. and boots £1 10s. The men were paid £1 4s. per annum. Coulings, the Chaldon Road corndealers, provided horses for fires and weekly practices at Townend Recreation Ground.

Caterham Fire Brigade, Coronation Year. 1911.

Fenton.

91. Captain Robert Vigar is sitting on the fire engine with his full complement of 12 part-time firemen in 1911. Six men were required to operate the manual fire engine, the other six fought the fire. Land for the Fire Engine House, still standing in the High Street, was leased from the School Board for one shilling per annum.

92. & 93.   At 5 a.m. on 2 May 1916, the Fire Brigade was summoned to the most disastrous fire Caterham had known. The *Old Surrey Hounds*, built before 1867, was ablaze. Starting in the cellar, the flames spread rapidly through the woodwork, the stock of spirits exploding. As the roof tiles were laid on straw, within one hour the roof collapsed, causing £2,000 worth of damage.

# School Days

The small National School in Chaldon Road founded by Lord of the Manor Thomas Clarke in 1816 'for the improvement of children' was the only school listed in the 1851 census returns. In 1914 there were two council schools, two church schools and five independent schools. Compulsory education together with the town's rapid expansion and attractive situation contributed to this increase in school places.

The state system was created by the 1870 Education Act, passed when Robert Lowe was Chancellor of the Exchequer. The elected parish School Board first met in December 1871 to provide undenominational education for the 299 Caterham children between five and 12 years. The National School building was converted to the Infants' School. In its grounds separate Boys' and Girls' Schools, the Headmaster's and Mistress' houses, designed by Richard Martin, built at a cost of £3,610, were opened on 2 July 1873. The Valley Mixed and Infants' Board Schools were built three years later. St John's Church School, housed since 1867 in two badly ventilated, inconvenient schoolrooms, moved in 1884 to its larger Godstone Road premises, the former temporary St John's church, formerly sited in Clareville Road. On the Hill, St Francis' Roman Catholic School progressed from a room opposite the *Golden Lion* in 1881 to the purpose built Essendene Road school in 1912.

These schools received government grants based on attainment and attendance, paid after the dreaded annual inspection. This system of payment by results, also promoted by Robert Lowe when Vice-President of the Committee of Council in Education, meant that most children learnt to read and write. For instance in St Mary's parish registers between 1837 and 1851, 21 out of 72 brides and grooms were unable to sign their names on the marriage certificate. Between 1900 and 1914 only four out of 704 could not do this. The practice led to a limited curriculum and did not prove a suitable basis for financing state schools. As School Boards were unable to provide suitable secondary education, Surrey County Council assumed responsibility for Caterham's education in 1903, appointing local managers. Board schools were renamed council schools. Howard Willmott Liversidge was the first Chairman of the Education Managers, while William Garland Soper was elected Vice-chairman of Surrey County Council's Education Committee.

Wealthier families preferred to send their children to private boarding schools, ideally in healthy surroundings. A succession of these opened and closed in the district. By 1861 the old coaching *Half Moon Inn* had been converted to Marden Lodge School, a boarding school for 13 young ladies. Twenty years later there were six similar establishments including the Dean School for young gentlemen. Only two schools have survived from the 19th century. Caterham School, originally the School for Sons of Congregational Ministers, transferred from Lewisham in 1884, and Eothen founded by the Misses Pye in 1892.

This is to Certify that *Henrietta Vigar*
was examined by Her Majesty's Inspector of Schools
*October 1878* and passed satisfactorily in the
subjects corresponding to Standard *III*
*William S. Soper, Chairman*

94. Ten-year-old blacksmith's daughter Henrietta Vigar was presented with this certificate at the annual School Board Tea and Prizegiving in January 1879. Every scholar in standards I to VI at the Hill Board School had been individually examined at the annual inspection. As the government grant depended on successful passes, the teaching was directed to achieving good results.

95.   Standard V taken outside the Hill Boys' School includes blacksmith's son, Tom Vigar (middle row, third left). A pupil teacher is standing on the left. The headmaster, George Rose, earning £100 per annum, was assisted by pupil teachers paid an annual salary of £12 during training. Recruited from the bright school leavers, they were taught by the headmaster and in turn taught the younger children.

96.   The Valley Mixed and Infants' Council Schools, Croydon Road, now the Adult Education Centre, were originally built at a cost of £2,800. Designed by School Board architect Richard Martin, they incorporated a school house for the Mistress. Opened on 10 January 1876, the school accommodated 150 pupils. By 1886 the Mistress, Mrs. Sarah Higgins, was assisted by an infants' mistress and four young pupil teachers.

97.   This delightful group of little girls attired in immaculate white pinafores and boys with starched collars includes Herbert (Bert) Douglas Holloway wearing a medal (back row fourth left). 'Caterham Valley Infts 1913' has been chalked on a classroom slate.

98. & 99.   Empire Day, 24 May, was celebrated with great enthusiasm. In 1913, over 1,000 children from the Guards' Depot, council, church and private schools marched to Timber Hill. Stirring hymns, including Rudyard Kipling's *Land of our Birth,* preceded saluting the Union Jack. The National Anthem was accompanied by the Guards' Depot Drum and Fife Band. In 1914, the venue was Queen's Park, the children from the Hill Council School can be seen passing the Fire Engine House in the High Street.

100.   The Hill Council School Orchestra, trained by their talented headmaster, Mr. G. Lonsdale (left), accompanied the patriotic songs at the 1914 Empire Day celebrations. On the following day, the orchestra was awarded the National Union of Orchestras' Shield, the first country school to win this contest, competed for by over 250 schools. The young violinists included Cyril Vigar, standing in the front row, first left. His cousin, George Ibbotson, is in the back row, fourth from the right.

101. The Roman Catholic school in Essendene Road was opened with due ceremony on 25 August 1912 by Bishop Amigo of Southwark after a service in the nearby church. The previous school, adjoining the Church of the Sacred Heart, had been condemned, so resourceful Father Roe hastily borrowed £1,000 from a fellow priest for the new building.

102. By 1871 The Villas, six identical four-storey semi-detached houses, had been built in Godstone Road. Ten years later, three properties had been converted to boarding schools. Nos.1 and 2, incorporated into the Hydro in 1898, was a girls' school in 1881. Next door, at No. 3 (left in this photograph), Henry Grinstead, the first Board School headmaster and later High Street postmaster, had opened a school for boys (*see* 130).

103.   The School for the Sons of Congregational Ministers (renamed Caterham School in 1912) moved to Withernden, Harestone Valley, in 1884. The house was originally Lake House, a private school designed by architect Richard Martin and built by local builder Robert Simmons. As this drawing by architect E. C. Robins demonstrates, Withernden, on the left, has been cleverly incorporated into the new school.

104.   The Congregational School's Prize Day on 31 July 1906 was presided over by George Croydon Marks J.P., M.P. After tea, Caterham Congregational minister, the Rev. Sydney Milledge, presented bibles to 17 school leavers, the Rev. Horace Hall, headmaster, gave his annual statement and Mrs. Marks presented the prizes. This postcard, published by Alec Braid, was sent to the Rev. T. Jones at Southampton by his schoolboy son.


105.   Eothen was founded by the Misses Catherine and Winifred Pye as a day school for local girls. In January 1892 eight pupils entered No. 2 West View, Harestone Hill. Five years later it was necessary to erect the school, seen on this postcard, on an adjacent field.

# Church & Chapel

On 11 August 1856, the 86-year-old rector, the Rev. James Legrew, was buried. His coffin was carried into the Norman church by eight parishioners wearing traditional white smocks. Since 1095, the tiny parish church had been large enough for the small population, but one week earlier, on 4 August, Caterham Railway had been formally opened. Within ten years the little church was redundant, replaced in 1866 by a larger church, more suitable for the fashionable gentry moving into the village.

The new Valley residents settling near the railway stations required churches within walking distance. In 1866, St Luke's church, Whyteleafe was consecrated, its parish including land from Caterham, Coulsdon and Warlingham parishes. In 1882, St John's church, Caterham Valley was built, replacing the temporary church used since 1872. William Garland Soper and other local Congregationalists attended the service and subscribed to the building fund, for co-operation between denominations was characteristic of Victorian Caterham. Their imposing church with its distinctive clock tower had been erected in 1875, superseding the small chapel in Stafford Road (later the Masonic Hall, now Stafford Hall). Between 1866 and 1884, over £33,000 was raised by generous worshippers for building and extending churches, providing over 2,000 additional seats.

Although the churches dispensed charity through their sick and needy funds, coal and clothing clubs, the working class, who could not afford pew rents and did not enjoy tedious sermons, preferred the lively evangelical chapels. The Valley Wesleyans had built their Croydon Road chapel in 1884 but the congregation dwindled in 1888 when the Plymouth Brethren met in nearby Bethany Hall, and faced further competition when the Salvation Army Citadel opened in 1907.

On the Hill, non-sectarian Oak Hall in Oak Road advertised 'Free Seats and No Collections' in the *Caterham Free Press* in 1894. Mission Halls near the Guards' Depot and Metropolitan Asylum had been established by St Mary's and the Congregational churches. The Guards' chaplains would preach at these services, but in 1901 the Wesleyan chaplain, the Rev. C. E. Mees, raised enough money to open modest Soldiers' Rooms at the corner of William Road. It was another chaplain, Father Roe, who was responsible for the Roman Catholic Church of the Sacred Heart although, unlike the other churches, this was not financed by public subscription, but by the Roe family.

Caterham, St. Lawrence Church

106. The ancient hill top-parish church, originally dedicated to St Leonard, consisted of a 26ft. x 15ft. nave with a small semi-circular Norman chancel at the east end. In the 13th century the chancel was extended by 12ft. and the north aisle added.

107. St Lawrence's church was only used as a Sunday school after St Mary's church, built on glebeland opposite, was consecrated in 1866. Its font and altar were transferred to St John's church. During restoration in 1927, the box pews seen in this 1903 photograph were removed and the ceiling taken down, exposing the original oak beams.

108. St Mary's church was planned for 550 worshippers but this was not achieved until the north aisle was completed in 1913. In 1883, when this drawing appeared in *The Builder*, the south aisle and chancel, tower and 126ft. spire were erected at a cost of £3,500. A carillon of bells was installed eight years later to commemorate Queen Victoria's Golden Jubilee.

109.   The attractive lychgate outside St Mary's church was dedicated before morning service on Sunday 12 April 1903. It was erected in memory of retired tea planter, John Shepard, who lived at Sylva House (*see* 36). A most generous benefactor to the church, his gifts included £400 to the 1883 building fund, a magic lantern for the Band of Hope in 1899 and £320 towards the new Parish Hall in 1901.

110.   St John's church tower with its four elegant spires, was described as a 'beacon of ornamentation' by the *Caterham Free Press* in its account of the dedication service on 26 June 1893. The tower completed the building programme, for the church, costing £16,000, designed by W. Bassett Smith, also architect of St Mary's church, had been consecrated on St John's Day, 27 December 1882.

111. Each summer 1,500 Anglican and Nonconformist families joined the parochial excursion organised by Henry Martin. On 20 June 1906, the resort was Hastings. At 7 a.m. two trains left the station, the first carrying the parents, the second with the children and Sunday School teachers. Paddling in the sea, steamer and charabanc trips, visits to the pier, castle and St Clements caves were all enjoyed.

112. The impressive Congregational church, designed by architect John Sulman, was situated on the corner of the Harestone estate. The land was donated by William Garland Soper who contributed handsomely to the building fund. The church was originally hidden by tall trees with a side gate in Harestone Hill, but the trees were felled and wrought-iron gates erected in 1911 so that the church would complement Soper Hall, then in the course of construction.

113. The Congregational church chose its ministers carefully, for not only had they to please the adult congregation but their sermons had to interest the College schoolboys who attended Sunday services. The three ministers in this unique photograph were excellent preachers, especially the Rev. Arthur Pringle whose eloquence filled the pews.

114.   These children belonged to the Junior Christian Endeavour Society attached to the Congregational Mission Hall, Coulsdon Road. They enjoyed weekly bible classes, lantern lectures, entertainments and outings. A popular national Nonconformist organisation, the Caterham Junior and Senior branches of it were started in 1893 by local builder William Thompson (*see* 30).

115. After the Anniversary Tea on 21 September 1892, the Treasurer, Mr. Lofthouse, announced that this weatherboarded Wesleyan chapel in Croydon Road, opened on 29 September 1884, was free from debt. Although saddler Edward Harris had donated the land, building expenses totalled £742. These had been repaid, not only by subscriptions from members and collections in other Wesleyan chapels, but by donations from the Congregational church and St John's church.

116. The Guards' Wesleyan church in Coulsdon Road was under the jurisdiction of the Wesleyan
Army & Navy Board until 1950. Completed in 1908 through the efforts of Guards' chaplain, the Rev.
C. E. Mees, who not only donated £500 but raised an additional £2,000, it was attached to the Soldiers'
Rooms and school chapel, which had opened in 1901.

117. Father Roe's wealthy family donated £5,000 in 1881 to build the Presbytery and Roman Catholic Church of the
Sacred Heart on the site of Shortfurrows farm. The church was not only used by guardsmen, but by parishioners
walking long distances to attend Sunday mass, as the parish extended to the Kent border.

118. The group photographed at the Guards' Wesleyan church garden party in 1909 includes members of the Jenner family. Mrs. Sarah Jenner is sitting with her small son Jack on her lap (third right). Her daughters Ruth and Doris, wearing pretty hats, are in front of her, while her husband is standing in the back row (second left).

# Medical Care

The first Cottage Hospital with five beds was opened on 23 August 1875 in Croydon Road, replacing a temporary building in Whyteleafe. It enabled working class patients of Dr. Ebenezer Diver, the only local practitioner, to receive adequate nursing care. By 3 June 1903, when a larger, better equipped hospital was formally opened by H.R.H. Princess Christian as a memorial to Queen Victoria, over 100 patients were admitted each year. Paid for by annual subscriptions and generous donations, organised by the Committee of Management, it was the only local charity to which the whole community contributed whatever their means.

After 1896, casualties could be given immediate attention by St John Ambulance Brigade members who transported serious cases by wheeled litter to the Cottage Hospital. Dental treatment was now available from qualified and registered dental surgeons, as a result of Sir John Tomes' foresight and endeavours. No kind of medical treatment was free, so thrifty working class men joined the Order of Foresters and other Friendly Societies. Their weekly contributions provided medical care at home and sickness payments when absent from work, while their colourful church parades raised money for the Cottage Hospital.

The unpopular Union workhouse at Bletchingley accommodated the destitute, although by 1914 conditions had improved in these institutions. The 1867 Metropolitan Poor Act, passed through Florence Nightingale's persistence, had aimed to alleviate the overcrowded insanitary wards in London workhouses by moving 'the quiet chronic insane and mentally defective' inmates to two identically built asylums at Leavesden, Hertfordshire and Caterham, each planned for 2,000 patients.

119.  Behind the Metropolitan Asylum's administrative offices, seen here, were the kitchen, bakery, laundry, gas works and waterworks. On the right is the recreation hall. Leading from these buildings, long corridors linked six blocks built for 1,000 male patients and seven blocks for 1,200 female patients cared for in large wards.

# METROPOLITAN ASYLUM DISTRICT.

### THE FOUNDATION STONE OF THIS ASYLUM ERECTED BY THE MANAGERS
### UNDER THE PROVISIONS OF THE METROPOLITAN POOR ACT 1867,
### WAS LAID BY
## D^R BREWER, M.P.
### CHAIRMAN OF THE BOARD
### ON SATURDAY THE 17^TH DAY OF APRIL 1869,

## COMMITTEE

WILLIAM S.CORTIS, ESQ^RE M.D CHAIRMAN.

| | |
|---|---|
| B.H.ADAMS, ESQ^RE | J.T.GRIFFITH, ESQ^RE M.D. |
| D^R BREWER, M.P. | B.POULTER, ESQ^RE |
| C.BURT, ESQ^RE | ALF^D SUTER, ESQ^RE } VICE CHAIRMAN OF THE BOARD |
| J.W.BUTTERWORTH, ESQ^RE | J.G.TALBOT, ESQ^RE M.P. |
| E.C.DANNELL, ESQ^RE | G.WILKINSON, ESQ^RE |

W.F.JEBB, ESQ^RE CLERK TO THE BOARD.

| ARCHITECTS, | CONTRACTOR, |
|---|---|
| JOHN GILES & BIVEN. | J.T.CHAPPELL. |

120.   The first 17 patients arrived at the Asylum 18 months after the foundation stone was laid. Its affairs were organised by the Committee of Management which held an annual inspection each summer. In 1887 it was reported in the *Croydon Chronicle* that 'the cost per head per day for the maintenance and clothing of patients was sixpence'.

121. The Asylum Band played at annual inspections and patients' and staff entertainments. Assistant medical officer Dr. J. F. Powell (front row, second left) can be seen in this 1912 Bunce Bros. photograph. Bandmaster Watts (middle row, first right) and other bandsmen wearing Asylum uniform were attendants. Former guardsmen from the adjoining Guards' Depot were still recruited for this work, although nursing lectures were given. In 1911 an Asylum Workers Union branch was formed.

122.   The laundresses were assisted by female patients in the Asylum Laundry as few labour-saving appliances were used. In 1901 a *Caterham Free Press* advertisement offered domestic staff £16 per annum plus 'board, lodging, washing and uniform and if desired £2.10s. a year in lieu of beer. 10s. a quarter allowed conditional on good behaviour'.

123. The farm and kitchen gardens not only provided food for the Asylum but occupation for the male patients. At the 1887 inspection 'a flock of healthy geese, assertive fowls, 35 well tended cows, 60 white and black pigs and nine fine horses were noticed. Three and a half cwt. of strawberries had been gathered and consumed in one day by the inmates' (*see* 15).

STAFF. NOV. 1918.

124.   This Cottage Hospital in Croydon Road served the community from 1875 to 1903. Although the number of beds had doubled from five to ten, the cases treated each year had risen from 17 to 108 during this period. Matron Smith and voluntary nurse Rolls, who opened their own nursing home in 1911, are photographed with patients before moving to the new hospital in 1903.

125.   There were 16 beds, an operating room and a hygienic kitchen on the ground floor of the new hospital. Staff bedrooms were provided on the first floor for the matron, two nurses and two servants. Opened in 1903 on a site adjacent to the first hospital, it boasted an up-to-date heating system and modern sanitary arrangements.

126. Mr Stripp's dogs, Floss and Nell, strategically sitting at the
bottom of the station ramp, collected £6 on Hospital Sunday,
6 July 1913. They chose their positions wisely for it rained heavily,
so marchers from 17 Friendly Societies, local fire brigades and
four bands were drenched during the colourful procession to St
John's church for the annual service.

127. Alfred Sergeant (1862-1915) was an indefatigable fund
raiser for the Cottage Hospital, not only collecting annual
subscriptions but organising the summer Hospital Saturday and
Sunday processions. He was employed as a decorator by builder
William Thompson. This photograph was taken outside his
Farningham Road house.

128. Jesse Hobson is photographed with his wife and six daughters outside his Commonwealth Road home *c*.1911. As he is wearing his Independent Order of Foresters' sash, he may have been attending a church parade in aid of the Cottage Hospital. A Caterham Urban District Council employee, his weekly payments to the Friendly Society provided his family with sickness benefits.

129. St John Ambulance Brigade members are standing in Queen's Park Road outside the Borer Memorial Ambulance Station on 13 January 1904. It was erected in memory of Brigade member Harry Borer who died in the Boer War. Alfred Riley, founder and later Caterham Superintendent, is photographed with his men, including blacksmith Robert Vigar, on the left.

130. By 1898 when local ironmonger John Burford opened the luxurious Hydro in Godstone Road, Caterham was already known for its healthy climate and pure water. The therapeutic baths were not only used by patients but patronised by local residents and visitors 'taking a cure' (*see* 102).

131.  The Garden Fete at Harestone on 17 July 1907 was the first event organised by the Caterham branch of the League of Mercy which made grants to voluntary hospitals. It was opened by Mrs. Soper, protected by her parasol. A pastoral play, tennis tournament, concert, sideshows, visits to the hot houses and dancing on the lawn were all enjoyed.

132. Sir John Tomes F.R.S., F.R.C.S., L.D.S. (1815-95) lived at Upwood Gorse, Tupwood Lane, his house designed by architect Philip Webb. He was the most eminent dental surgeon of his age. By his efforts, dentistry became a recognised branch of medicine and a registration system was instituted. His *System of Dental Surgery* published in 1859 became a standard textbook. Knighted in 1886, he is buried in Caterham cemetery.

133. Mr. Shipley Slipper, a registered surgeon-dentist, inserted notices in the *Caterham Free Press*, drawing attention to his surgeries in Caterham and Redhill. In this advertisement, dated 4 June 1892, it seems somewhat inappropriate that a room in a confectioner's shop should be rented for the monthly surgery.

# The Social Scene

'Caterham Gardeners & Cottagers Mutual Improvement Society', founded in 1878, was a typical Victorian society. Its initial object was to arrange fortnightly horticultural lectures. An early secretary was Robert Catt, Metropolitan Asylum head gardener. A treasurer was William Garland Soper. The annual shows were financed by wealthy vice-presidents and subscribers concerned with educating the working classes. At the 35th Annual Show at Harestone in 1913, gardeners from the large estates won challenge cups, cottagers exhibited vegetables, parlourmaids arranged centrepieces, nurserymen mounted elaborate displays, tradesmen paraded smart horse and delivery carts and the United Band played. Local people attended in large numbers for, with no cheap reliable transport, entertainments within walking distance were well-patronised.

The Fur and Feather Fanciers' Club held its annual shows in the commodious but draughty Public Hall, Godstone Road. This was the venue for exhibitions, sales of work, concerts and plays, often in aid of the Cottage Hospital, although in wet weather voices were drowned by rain on the corrugated roof. Naturalist Richard Kearton would give lectures illustrated by lantern slides or moving pictures. The Masonic Hall, Harestone Hall, the Institute and St Mary's Parish Hall were filled to capacity for University Extension lectures, Sunday afternoon penny readings, debates and poetry readings.

By 1914 social activities were changing. Mass entertainment had arrived in the town when the two cinemas opened. A bus service and cheap evening train tickets meant that leisure could be spent in Croydon or London with their more sophisticated attractions.

# CATERHAM

## Industrial, Fine Art & Loan Exhibition,

### 1893.

### ⋙ WHITSUN WEEK, ⋘

### MAY 23rd, 24th, 25th, and 26th.

## Public Hall, Caterham Valley.

President: The Right Honourable LORD HYLTON, J.P., D.L.

**[CATALOGUE.]**

### Admission :

TUESDAY AFTERNOON, Two Shillings and Sixpence; EVENING, One Shilling.

WEDNESDAY ⎫
THURSDAY ⎬ AFTERNOON, One Shilling; EVENING, Sixpence.
FRIDAY ⎭

**CHILDREN UNDER TWELVE HALF PRICE.**

134. Over 4,000 people from Caterham and the surrounding villages visited the four-day Industrial, Fine Art and Loan Exhibition organised by Henry Martin in 1893. They viewed valuable paintings and engravings loaned by the Corporation of London, together with family portraits, silver, samplers, medals, Roman antiquities, geological specimens and foreign curiosities exhibited by local residents in the Public Hall.

THERE WILL BE ON VIEW IN THE HALL A

# MILITARY ENCAMPMENT,

CONSISTING OF

## "Tortoise," Officers' and Bell Tents,

Fully fitted as for Service, together with

### CAMEL AND PACK-HORSE, laden with Stores, etc.

### NATIVE BEARERS AND ATTENDANTS, etc.,

THE WHOLE ARRANGED BY

CAPTAIN A. SAVILL TOMPKINS,

HOLMWOOD, CATERHAM.

---

# NATURAL HISTORY COLLECTION,

ARRANGED AS

# A JUNGLE,

AND COMPRISING

| | | |
|---|---|---|
| LION | OUNCE OR SNOW LEOPARD | CHEETAH |
| LEOPARD | KANGAROO | ALLIGATOR |
| BEARS | BRIDGE OF MONKEYS | BIRDS, &c. |

Also a CAMEL, with Monkey Driver,

POLAR BEARS, &c.

The above lent and arranged by

MR. J. HIGHT BLUNDELL,

BRYNTIRION, STANSTEAD.

---

# ❖ A Stall for Sale of Work ❖

WILL BE OPENED

## IN AID OF THE EXHIBITION FUNDS.

# REFRESHMENTS

Under the management of Mr. G LOVITT, Caterham.

TEAS WILL BE PROVIDED.

135.  Captain Savill Tompkin's Military Encampment and Mr. Hight Blundell's Jungle were popular attractions at the 1893 Exhibition. Entertainments were given by the Valley Brass & Reed Band and Board School choirs. In St John's School over 400 handmade articles were judged in the Industrial Exhibition and 150 contestants entered the cookery and carpentry competitions.

136. The Red Indian play *Wahonomin* was 'performed by a number of young ladies and gentlemen' to an enthusiastic audience at the Public Hall on Saturday afternoon 11 January 1913, in aid of the Girls' Diocesan Association. The Urban Electric Supply Co. provided the stage lighting. This flashlight photograph of the cast was taken by Bunce Bros.

137. The Skating Carnival at the Public Hall was a colourful affair with the skaters and dancers in fancy dress. Miss Williams won the ladies' prize as a Dutch boy and Mr. Burnett, as a Michelin tyre, won the gentlemen's prize. Chinese lanterns illuminated by electricity were much praised. The roller skating sessions held twice weekly in 1909 had proved so popular that a new maple floor had been laid in December.

138.  Caterham Silver Band was one of several bands in existence before 1908. Rivals included the Caterham Brass Band and the Valley Reed & Brass Band. Finally they all amalgamated in 1908, forming the Caterham United Silver Band. By 1911 this new band was winning challenge cups at important band competitions.

139. Visitors to the 1907 Horticultural Show at Essendene included Mrs. Alice Frankland with baby daughter Violet in the pushchair and three-year-old Charlie by her side. They would have visited the hot houses and gardens, viewed Burntwood gardener Mr. C. Lane's prize-winning fruit and vegetables in the competitors' marquee and admired nurseryman Rayner Hill's floral lighthouse.

140. Essendene gardener Mr. J. Brand received the coveted Challenge Cup, donated by Mr. E. H. Coles of Burntwood, at the 1909 Horticultural Show held at Portley. In this Bunce Bros. photograph, members include: (left to right) back row – , J. Brand, F. Brazier, W. Appleton, R. Vigar, Mr. Taylor; third row standing S. Toop, P. Broad, – , A. Wood, W. Thompson, H. Groves, – , W. Toms; seated C. Lane, – , – , – , W. Brind (Secretary), F. Young, R. Catt; front row J. Molyneux, – , – .

141.   At the 1913 Horticultural Show held at Harestone, a Baby Show was introduced with three classes. The *Caterham Weekly Press* reported that prizes were won by 'Mrs Budd – under six months; Mrs. Bangs – six to eighteen months; Mrs. Force – twins under eighteen months'.

142.   The Horse Parade was a popular event at both the Horticultural Society and Fanciers' Club shows. As many as 50 tradesmen would parade through the town prior to judging. At the 1913 Horticultural Show, first prize, donated by Mr. C. Nichols of Upwood Tower, was won by Valley coal merchants Gladden Bros. in the 'tradesmen's heavy turnout class'.

143.  The ninth annual Fanciers' Club Show in October 1901 at the Public Hall produced 1,266 entries. Poultry, pigeons, rabbits, cats, cavies, mice and cage birds were shown. Frederick Hawkins of Chestnut Lodge, Addison Road, a second prize winner for his Rhode Island Red hen, was presented with a joint of meat donated by Valley poulterer G. H. Jones.

144.  The 1902 Fanciers' Club Show committee were (left to right): standing C. Jarrett, – , C. Crees, J. Palmer, R. G. Knight, W. Kilby, A. Haydon; seated H. Freeman, J. Kilby (Secretary), J. D. Rolls (Chairman), A. Dunn. Livery stables proprietor, William Kilby, not only won 10 prizes for his pigeons at this show, but awards at the Peterborough, Okehampton, Gravesend, Fareham and Northallerton shows.

145.   Caterham Institute, founded in 1894 by the Rev. Fergus Wood, vicar of St John's church, moved into the premises on the left, vacated by the *Coffee Tavern*. The attraction on opening night, 26 November 1902, attended by over 100 members, was the full-size slate billiard table in the first-floor games room. The reading room and lending library, with books donated by the president Percy Clarke, were on the second floor.

146.   Richard Kearton F.Z.S., F.R.P.S. (1862-1928), the eminent naturalist, author, photographer and lecturer, born at Thwaite in Swaledale, Yorkshire, moved to Caterham in 1898. He is seen here felling a tree with his sons Dick, Jack and Cherry in his garden at Ashdene, Croydon Road in 1909. Each winter he travelled extensively, giving popular natural history lectures illustrated with his own lantern slides and, later, moving films.

147. Richard Kearton, seen here supporting his equally famous brother, Cherry, photographing a small bird, pioneered natural history photography. There were no telephoto lenses, so he would spend many hours sitting patiently in cleverly constructed hides. His three sons would help him carry his heavy and unwieldy camera equipment and glass negatives to Great Dene and Birchwood (now Kearton Nature Reserve).

148.  'Humorous, mirth provoking and instructive cinematograph exhibitions' were shown at the Electric Theatre, converted from a disused coach builder's premises adjoining the *Blacksmiths Arms*. Mr. Freeman of Chepstow Hall, Peckham, not only hired films for the fascinated audience but showed his own productions in 1910.

# ELECTRIC THEATRE,
## High Street, CATERHAM HILL.

Continuous Programme from 7 till 11 on Wednesday, Thursday, Friday and Saturday Evenings.

*Highly Refined Attractive Entertainment.*
Free from Vulgarity.   Adapted alike for Child or Adult.

Open for Private Exhibition on the last four afternoons of the week

MATINEES  WEDNESDAY  AFTERNOONS  at 3.
CHILDREN'S  MATINEES  on  SATURDAYS  at  2.30,
Admission Half-price.

ADMISSION  3d.          RESERVED  TIP  SEATS,  6d.

149.   The Valley Cinema opened on 7 July 1913 in the assembly room behind the *Commonwealth Tavern*, a public house converted from two cottages in 1866. Bowler-hatted licensee George Gammon is standing outside. He had hired from Pathe Freres, for the week beginning 12 January 1914, *The Rosary, Broncho Billy and the Schoolmam's Sweetheart*, the serial *Whatever happened to Mary* and comic film *Bingles and the Cabaret*.

# The Sporting Life

The first sporting event recorded in Caterham took place on 14 October 1767. The cricketing 'gentlemen of Catterham', captained by Henry Rowed of Caterham Court, wearing his famous gold laced hat, unexpectedly beat invincible Hambledon from Hampshire. The series of cricket matches played by these teams between 1767 and 1770 drew record crowds. Reputedly 20,000 spectators saw Hambledon beat Caterham in August 1769 at Guildford.

It was not until a hundred years later that generous patrons once more moved into the village, willing to buy equipment, donate prizes and entertain club members. In addition, facilities were provided at the Metropolitan Asylum and Guards' Depot. Cricket and football teams were formed and fixtures arranged. Opponents included Caterham Park and the Wednesday afternoon Early Closers Cricket Clubs, whose home grounds were Queen's Park or the Dene cricket ground. The Rectory field was used by the Caterham Park Football Club whose headquarters were the Village Club. The popular Cycling Club met there in the winter, while their annual race meetings were held at the cricket ground as there was no track in Queen's Park. However, a bowling green, proposed by Bowling Club President Cllr. Edmund Perry, was laid in the park after many objections, including protests in the *Caterham Weekly Press* 'against the proposed confiscating of ratepayers' property for practically private purposes'.

There was no opposition to Caterham Rifle Club formed in 1907. After the inaugural public meeting chaired by William Garland Soper, patriotic gentlemen, ladies, tradesmen, working class men, boy scouts and schoolboys learned to shoot at the Waller Lane rifle range donated by Robert Turner J.P. Its first annual meeting in October 1908 was a grand affair, for Secretary of State for War, the Rt. Hon. Robert Haldane, distributed the valuable prizes and certificates in a packed Public Hall.

150.   The Village Club, Townend (now the British Legion), was financed by Lloyd's underwriter Henry Poland. It opened on 11 October 1902 to 'provide healthy amusement for men who did not wish to go to public houses'. Equipped with a gymnasium, reading, recreation and billiard rooms, it was the headquarters of the Village C.C., Caterham Park F.C. and Caterham Cycling Club whose badge is underneath the right-hand window.

151. Caterham Cycling Club founder, and President, Henry Poland, and his wife are flanked by members wearing their club badges on caps or lapels. Wednesday and Saturday evening or Sunday all day runs were organised to the coast or nearby towns. The winter programme included training sessions at the Village Club and smoking concerts at their President's home, Greenlands, Buxton Lane (now Buxton Lodge Nursing Home).

152. The race meetings organised by Caterham Cycling Club, founded in 1894, were held on the Dene field. The Council roller was used beforehand to prepare the track. The Three Mile Club Championship race was rarely without incident as more than one leader was toppled off his machine just before the winning post.

153.  Cricket matches were sociable affairs. At this match on the Dene field, afternoon tea is being prepared for players and spectators. The cricketers would have already enjoyed a good lunch at a local hostelry and would be looking forward to a convivial dinner followed by a 'capital entertainment'.

154. The annual entertaining Whips and Wheels *v.* Worms cricket match took place on the Dene cricket ground. On 19 August 1912, 14 coachmen and chauffeurs played 12 gardeners. In spite of being outnumbered, the gardeners who had only lost two matches since 1881, won again by 70 runs.

155. St Lawrence's Lads Club football team, members of St Mary's Bible Class, won the Edenbridge and District League championship in 1912. Coached by the curate, the Rev. Maurice Daniell, players included prolific scorer Jack Smith (front row left). Trained at the Village Club, the champions were presented with a handsome shield by the President, Henry Poland, on 4 November at the Annual General Meeting.

156. Caterham Bowling Club was officially opened twice. After the first ceremony in Queen's Park on Whit Monday 5 June 1911, shown here, the green was ruined by abnormally hot weather and angry resident James Balch. Incensed by turves from Townend Recreation Ground being used, he removed them on several occasions. After Councillor E. J. Syer donated 600 new turves, the club re-opened on 30 April 1913.

157. The Old Surrey Hounds hunted on Tuesdays and Saturdays. The huntsmen would assemble in The Square after riding down from Tillingdown into Timber Hill to use the horse trough outside the *Old Surrey Hounds* public house. Blacksmith Robert Vigar seated on his horse (right) would join them on Saturday afternoons after a busy working week.

158. Lady golfers, including Lorna Herbert of Torwood (seated second left) and her sister, Muriel (seated fourth left), are photographed on 26 April 1911 outside the Warlingham Golf Club house. The name is misleading for the club was opened in 189 on the Caterham Manor estate with the Manor House as its club house.

159. In October 1904 it was reported in the *Caterham Weekly Press* that 'the Old Surrey Hounds (25½ couples) are kenelled at Kenley'. The puppies were trained by members such as Robert Vigar (left) who received a coveted cup for 'puppy walking'.

160. In 1911 Caterham Rifle Club, founded in 1907, won the Sheriff's Shield presented for competition among the Godstone Union Rifle Clubs. The winning team comprised H. W. Cox, T. Diprose, J. W. Gorham, W. Payn, J. Sheldon and A. Taylor. Their rifles bearing the inscription 'Entirely British', were ex-military Martini-Henry *c*.1870, converted to .22in. calibre by Messrs. W. W. Greener. They would have been donated to the Rifle Club by a wealthy vice-president (*see* 162).

# Army Life

In 1887 the Garrison chapel at the Guards' Depot and the Public Hall in Godstone Road, used for drill by the local Volunteers, both paid for by subscription, were opened. These reflected the Victorians' pride in the professional army and the civilian Volunteers.

The I Company of the 1st Battalion of Surrey Volunteers (The Queen's) Royal West Surrey Regiment, raised in 1885, was one of seven companies in the Croydon area. By 1887 there were 110 Volunteers under the command of Captain Timmis, of The Beeches, Church Hill, a civil engineer by profession. Viscount Sherbrooke, Major General Sibley, William Garland Soper and John Shepard not only subscribed two guineas a year to the Volunteers, but bought debenture shares in the Public Hall Company.

The Volunteers, like the Rifle Club, benefited from the transfer of the Guards' Depot for training Grenadier, Coldstream and Scots Guards' recruits, from Warley, Essex to Caterham. The 22-acre site adjoining the Metropolitan Asylum was purchased for £6,312 in 1875, after the original proposal to move to Croydon was abandoned due to considerable local opposition. By October 1877 when the first recruits arrived by train, £46,273 had been spent on the buildings. The officers' mess and quarters, sergeants' mess and canteen, their married quarters and the recruits' four two-storey barrack blocks with cookhouse had been completed. Within the high perimeter wall were also found the hospital, schoolroom, carpenters' and shoemakers' block, quartermaster's stores and guardroom.

In 1881, 503 soldiers and their families stationed in the Depot were listed in the census returns. The 299 recruits from every county were being disciplined and drilled by Superior Barracks Sergeant Edward Alcock with assistance from three drill sergeants and 27 instructors. Six school teachers were making up deficiencies in the recruits' board school education. As a direct result of army reforms following the Crimean War, serious attempts were made to improve the men's welfare. Early visitors to the Depot commented favourably on the N.C.O.s' reading and recreation rooms, skittles alley and weekly entertainments.

Commandants encouraged local initiative in providing additional amenities for the troops such as the non-denominational Soldiers' Homes in the High Street. In return Caterham received visits from H.R.H. Duke of Connaught, T.R.H. Duke and Duchess of Argyll, Lord Wolseley and Lord Roberts to lay foundation stones, open buildings and support fund raising bazaars. Leading residents shared the same platform or luncheon table. Tradesmen patriotically decorated their shops.

Relations between town and Depot were always satisfactory, in spite of 12 public houses within walking distance. Cricket and football matches were played and boxing tournaments arranged, dinners were held in the sergeants' mess and the annual Flower Show enjoyed by local families. St Mary's parish registers record 125 army marriages between 1877 and 1914, while guardsmen, trained at the Depot, have settled in the town after completing their service.

161. Village blacksmith Robert Vigar was sworn in by Major General Sibley at the first meeting of the Volunteers in 1885. A talented musician, he was soon promoted to bandmaster. The 1st Volunteer Battalion wearing their smart red uniforms played at military and social functions including the 1887 and 1897 Caterham Jubilee celebrations.

162. Arthur Taylor, photographed in his Volunteer's uniform, was an expert shot. He is surrounded by some of his many prizes. A founder member of the Rifle Club, he took part in local competitions (see 160). Head gardener at Sylva House, he lived in Sylva Cottage, Waller Lane (now Rose Cottage).

163.  Sergeant Arthur Taylor is seated (centre) with fellow Volunteers in the Drill or Public Hall in 1906. In July 1913 it was sold by the Public Hall Co. to the War Office although social events were still held there.

164.  The splendidly decorated Soldiers' Home in the High Street, costing £1,500, was designed by Henry Martin. Opened by Field Marshal Lord Roberts on 28 October 1898, there was a ground-floor billiard room, a spacious first-floor room for Saturday entertainments, games and recreation rooms together with a non-alcoholic refreshment bar for use by off-duty guardsmen. Second-floor bedrooms were reserved for soldiers' relatives. Miss Mary Duncan, the Presbyterian chaplain's daughter, is seen flanked by her 'boys'. Appointed Superintendent in 1909, she retired in 1942.

165.  The four Guards' Depot chaplains were trustees of the Soldiers' Home. This unique photograph taken *c*.1905 demonstrates their joint concern for the men's welfare. Standing: left, Father F. Roe (Roman Catholic); right, Rev. J. C. W. Tuckey (Church of England). Seated: left, Rev. C. E. Mees (Wesleyan); right, Rev. J. Duncan (Presbyterian). A stained glass window in the Guards' Depot chapel records the friendship between the Wesleyan and Anglican chaplains.

166.  Old English Fair, organised by the lady subscribers to pay off the Soldiers' Home's outstanding mortgage, was graciously opened by H.R.H. Princess Louise, Duchess of Argyll. Messrs. Whiteley, the London 'universal providers', transformed the cavernous Public Hall into picturesque 'Old English Market Place'. The stall holders wore elaborate medieval costumes.

*Merrie England*

# OLD ENGLISH FAIR

*PUBLIC HALL, CATERHAM,*

*IN AID OF THE SOLDIERS' HOME, 1st & 2nd DECEMBER, 1911*

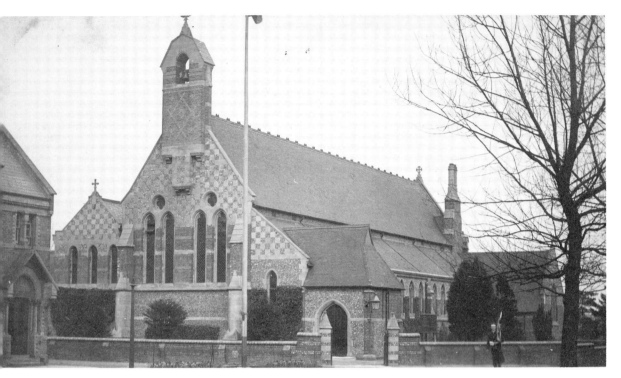

167. A simple memorial in the entrance to the Guards' Depot chapel, dedicated on 16 February 1887, records that it was built 'mainly through the munificence of Lt. General Philip Smith C.B. who commanded the Grenadier Guards and afterwards the Home District'. As the War Office would only contribute £3,000, he raised the remaining £5,000. This chapel seated 550, and the north aisle was reserved for Roman Catholic services.

168. Sunday morning church parade was compulsory. Anglican troops attended services in the Guards' Depot chapel, but Nonconformists marched to the nearby Congregational or Wesleyan chapels. As lunch was served at 12 o'clock sharp, more than one long-winded preacher was astonished to see the congregation leaving in the middle of the sermon.

169.   Repeated drills and tough physical exercise during their initial training turned the young raw recruits into immaculate disciplined troops. Inspections were conducted by officers or distinguished visitors. Nearly 1,000 recruits assembled on the parade ground during H.R.H. Duke of Connaught's visit in 1904. Behind the guards are A Block married quarters built for 14 families in 1877.

170.   The Drum and Fife Band can be seen at the far end of the front row in plate 168. It provided music on military occasions as there was no military band at the Depot. On Sunday 29 October 1899, when the first contingent of guardsmen left by train to join their regiments for service in the Boer War, the Drum and Fife Band played patriotic music outside the station where an enormous crowd had gathered.

CATERHAM. Guard's Depot                    Drums & Fifes

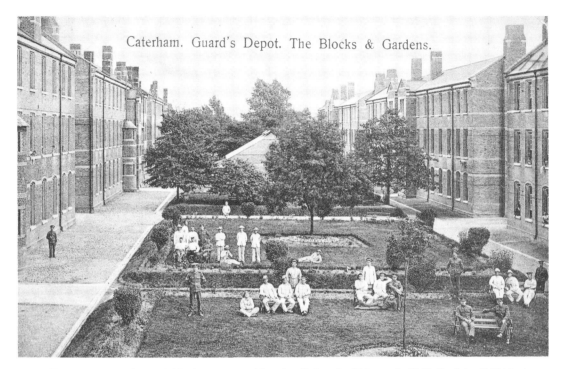

171. Four two-storey barrack blocks were considered sufficient for 500 men in 1877. By 5 April 1900 when the Irish Guards were formed, two more three-storey blocks had been built and an extra floor added to the original blocks. The gardens between the blocks where the guardsmen are relaxing were tended by N.C.O.s and trained soldiers.

172. Sergeant Chaddock's squad outside their barrack block can be recognised as Scots guardsmen by their checkered cap bands and tunic button arrangement. Although this is one of photographer Fenton's Coronation year souvenirs, squad pictures were his stock in trade (*see* 91 & 164). With trained recruits frequently leaving the Depot to join their regiments, there was a continual demand for such photographs.

*Parade at the Guard's Depôt, Caterham.*

173. Declaration of War on Tuesday 4 August 1914 marked the end of an era for both Caterham and the Guards' Depot. By the next afternoon the recruits had joined their battalions but, by the end of August, they had been replaced by 4,000 wartime recruits arriving unexpectedly at the Depot gates. This created severe problems with accommodation, sanitation and food. As many as 600 new volunteers would arrive at Caterham station each day, trudging wearily up Waller Lane after long journeys from the Midlands, North, Scotland and Ireland. Conditions are vividly captured by Bunce Bros. in this last photograph. The cricket field doubles as a second parade ground, tents have been hastily pitched and the first temporary huts are being erected.

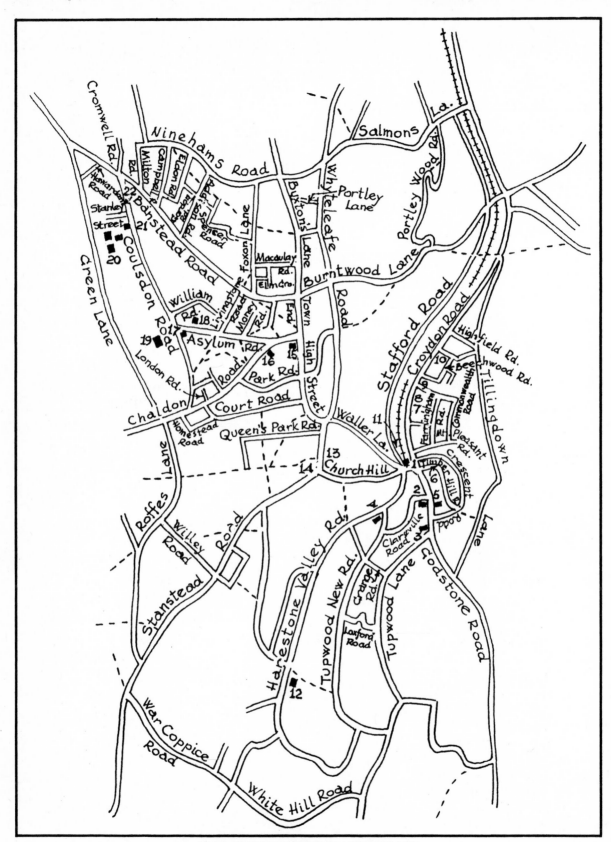

**1911 CENSUS FOR CATERHAM**